IMAGES
of America

SCHAUMBURG'S WOODFIELD MALL

I0809480

On the cover: This image provides an aerial view of Schaumburg's Woodfield Mall as it appeared in 1981. Absent from the photograph are the Zurich Towers to the west of the water tower, Woodfield Village Green shopping strip on the north side of Golf Road, and Streets of Woodfield to the south of Woodfield Road. In place of all missing structures are open fields, which is a rare sight in 2006. (Courtesy of Voice of Schaumburg Collection/Schaumburg Township District Library.)

IMAGES
of America

SCHAUMBURG'S WOODFIELD MALL

William J. Holderfield

ARCADIA
PUBLISHING

Copyright © 2007 by William J. Holderfield
ISBN 978-0-7385-5102-9

Published by Arcadia Publishing
Charleston, South Carolina

Printed in the United States of America

Library of Congress Control Number: 2007922781

For all general information contact Arcadia Publishing at:
Telephone 843-853-2070
Fax 843-853-0044
E-mail sales@arcadiapublishing.com
For customer service and orders:
Toll-Free 1-888-313-2665

Visit us on the Internet at www.arcadiapublishing.com

This book was not sponsored, endorsed, prepared, or published by Woodfield Mall LLC, the Taubman Company LLC, or any of their owners, affiliates, partners, managers, employees, or operators. Woodfield Mall LLC and the Taubman Company LLC make no representations as to the accuracy of any statements made herein. All opinions and views are exclusively those of the author.

To Kelly, for putting up with yet another stack of papers and books. To Kitty and Peanut for keeping me sane on this journey.

Contents

ACKNOWLEDGMENTS

I wish to thank the Sears archivist Arlene May. Thanks to J. C. Penney archivist Jane Gosnell at Southern Methodist University. Thanks to the Schaumburg Township District Library (STDL) and Schaumburg Township Historical Society archivist Jane Rozek for allowing me a large amount of time to peruse the photograph catalogs and space to scan all the images. Additional thanks go to the director of the STDL, Michael Madden, for allowing me to use the photographs at the library in the publication. Thanks also to those other departments at the STDL that afforded so much help and time.

Thanks to H. Robert Baker of Georgia State University and Chris Chulos of Roosevelt University for their support on this project and all things history related. Thanks to Leon Stein, Celeste Chamberland, Regina Buccola, Steve Cohen, and Bruce Kraig for all the support and knowledge provided in order to make this book possible. Additional thanks go to all faculty and staff at Roosevelt University for helping me become the student I am today.

Thanks to Gavin Kleespies, director of the Mount Prospect Historical Society, for the materials and support provided on this project. A special thanks goes to Gavin for the chance to begin my historical research career as a volunteer with the historical society. Much research for this book was culled from archived articles from the *Chicago Tribune*.

And of course a big thanks to Arcadia Publishing and my editor, Jeff Ruetsche, and John Pearson for all the help on this book, as well as for dealing with my various issues and deadlines.

I also wish to thank my parents for providing me with an education and an interest in history. Thanks to my grandparents for their support in all things historical and especially during my first graduate course at Roosevelt University. Finally I wish to thank my wife, Kelly, for the ability to do what I enjoy; and the love of our family that helped keep my stress level low and the drive to complete the book high.

Introduction

The Schaumburg area was settled in 1835, not long after the United States and local Native American tribes signed the Treaty of Chicago in 1833, which did not take effect until 1835. With the removal of the Native Americans from Illinois, land was open for settlement. The draw of settlement in the vicinity of Chicago was inevitable given the access to Lake Michigan. The land outside the limits of Chicago was another possibility altogether. As land speculation was in full swing, many New Yorkers were looking to buy land in the west, and the area outside of Chicago was one such place.

The prospect of large tracts of land to settle on and start a new life for many German immigrants was a great opportunity. The first settlers in most of what are today's towns and villages were of German descent, or came from the New York area. Schaumburg was no exception. Ernst Schween and Johann Sunderlage were two such settlers. In addition to the German population, others began to come to the Schaumburg area around 1835, the same time that Schween and Sunderlage settled on their land. Trumball Kent of New York settled on land in the northeast portion of Schaumburg Township, while Horace Williams, another New Yorker, owned portions of land in the area of Schaumburg, despite living in what is today Palatine. By 1836, Sunderlage had brought his family and friends from Germany to this new territory to settle the land with him. Much of the land that his friends and family settled became Schaumburg and Hoffman Estates. However, it was not until 1842 that these early settlers gained the deed to their land with the federal land sales taking place for the area they occupied. By 1870, Schaumburg was completely German because other settlers that had come in the 1830s, 1840s, and 1850s moved further west and sold their land to German immigrants and descendants in the area.

In 1850, the name put forth by Frederick Nerge, another early German settler, during a town meeting was Schaumburg and the name stuck due to many family ties to the area known in Germany as Schaumburg-Lippe. Not surprisingly, Schaumburg-Lippe would become the sister city of Schaumburg in later years. By the late 1850s, as many towns had begun to spring up in what is today's Chicago Northwest Suburbs, a town center and marketplace were established for farmers in the area. As the marketplace grew, a need for additional services and business opportunities arose. Cobblers, blacksmiths, shopkeepers, and other such businesses came to existence in the area near what are today Schaumburg Road and Roselle Road.

Schaumburg was unlike any of the other local communities. Towns such as Des Plaines, Mount Prospect, Arlington Heights, and Palatine were created much in the same way as Schaumburg during the mid-1800s, but Schaumburg grew in size by different means. These other suburbs would begin to expand in the 1850s in size and population as train stations were erected for the Illinois and Wisconsin Railroad, which today is known as the Chicago and North Western Railway, to stop along its run. Schaumburg did not have the benefit of the railroad to help build its community or take part in commerce with Chicago. As a result, Schaumburg remained a small town and farming community until the mid-1950s.

The only shopping center available to the suburban population, with rare visits to Chicago for shopping, was the town general store. This was the first mall. The general store had various items available and was the one exception to the specialty stores that existed for such things as blacksmiths and cobblers. The general store was a combination clothing store, grocery store, and hardware store. The items sold were things that were not obtainable through a farmers market or made in the home, items that could spend a significant period of time on the shelf until purchased by locals. As the town grew in size, more stores were added, which also began to include saloons, restaurants, and hotels by the early part of the 20th century, servicing about 1,000 residents.

During this period, the only way to travel to Schaumburg was by horse and wagon, until automobiles became available to the public. However, Schaumburg was too far away from the train stations of surrounding towns and Chicago, making the area reliant on farmwork until the 1950s. With the trains of other towns growing in popularity for weekend excursions, as the *Chicago Tribune* reported in 1853, many city dwellers could venture into the suburbs to see the rural sights and have a picnic in the country. Many would move to the areas near the train depots to take up residence while still working in Chicago. The growth in commuters in the suburbs prompted changes in the size, structure, and purpose of the train stations, moving them from depots for goods to be picked up or dropped off to being a place for pedestrians to wait for their way to work. In the city of Chicago the same changes were taking place, creating the Chicago and North Western Railway station in Chicago with three levels to accommodate the large number of suburban workers in 1911. By the 1920s, the stations were being built less frequently and in smaller sizes in the outlying areas.

The rise of the automobile began to be a means to travel from the suburbs to Chicago. However, Schaumburg remained a farming community. The first paved roads appeared in Schaumburg in 1920, with the paving of Higgins Road and Roselle Road, and by 1928 Golf Road would be paved. It was not until 1954 that the Northwest Tollway was proposed, thanks to the highway system plan of Pres. Dwight D. Eisenhower. On a 1956 map by Paul Baldwin, the Northwest Tollway was marked as the toll road and was labeled as a planned road. This same year the first mayor of Schaumburg, Louis Redeker, was elected not long after the Village of Schaumburg was incorporated on March 7, 1956. The incorporated area covered approximately two square miles and contained 130 residents around the town center of Schaumburg Road and Roselle Road.

Schaumburg would slowly grow in size thanks to the completion of the Northwest Tollway and the opening of O'Hare Airport in 1955 to commercial flights, with the majority of flights being diverted to O'Hare from Midway by 1962. By 1959, Schaumburg would elect Robert O. Atcher. Atcher would help create the Schaumburg that many experience today, despite retiring in 1975. With Atcher as mayor, the first large-scale subdivision would be built by Alfred Campanelli in 1959; it would become known as Weathersfield. In 1961, Schaumburg adopted a five-year plan that was proposed by planning consultants. Since Schaumburg was incorporated in 1956, it held the ability to expand in size and a lot of land was available for incorporation.

One

First Regional Mall

Located near Schaumburg, Mount Prospect, a "railroad town", was incorporated in 1917. By 1956, Mount Prospect had seen the need to erect a regional mall in order to gain the necessary business-related taxes and sales taxes that would allow it to keep from collecting taxes from home owners to pay for roads and municipality expenses. This was the direction that many suburbs were taking at this time. A move to collect property taxes was inevitable to accommodate a growing village and hopefully a growing population. The only other option to keep from collecting property taxes or to curb increasing costs of property taxes, which angered many citizens in the suburbs of Chicago, was to shift the cost elsewhere, which included sales tax.

Mount Prospect proposed building the Mount Prospect Plaza in the center of town, with a Randhurst Shopping Center mall being proposed on the periphery of the village. The village, like Schaumburg, was able to annex outlying land because it was incorporated, which Mount Prospect did to farmland to the northeast of its boundaries. Mount Prospect Plaza opened in 1962 with Goldblatt's Department Store as the anchor. However, Mount Prospect Plaza was just a strip mall. It was Randhurst Shopping Center that would revolutionize the industry of shopping. Famous Austrian developer Victor Gruen was given the task of creating this mall. The Randhurst Corporation would take charge of the financial backing, and its parent company store, Carson Pirie Scott, would be one of the major anchor stores of the newly erected mall. Randhurst Shopping Center would open on the periphery of Mount Prospect, pulling business and later housing, from the center of town. The other anchor stores would be Wieboldt's and the Fair. Randhurst would be triangular, with each anchor store at a different end of the mall and a dome covering the center of the mall. Randhurst would hold two floors and, with one million square feet of space, the largest enclosed shopping center in the Midwest and the largest air-conditioned shopping center in the nation.

This is an artist's sketch of the interior of Randhurst Mall before construction began. The idea of having a lounging area or food court in the center of the mall was something that was anticipated as a feature of Randhurst Mall. This drawing does not contain any visible stores and looks more like an office building complete with men in suits. (Courtesy of the Mount Prospect Historical Society.)

This image shows Victor Gruen looking over a model of his creation. The triangular shape of Randhurst Mall marks his unique idea of creating three anchor stores with a straight walkway of fanfare between each of the stores. The center of the mall, given its special trademark dome, was to be a center of congregation for shoppers and the community. (Courtesy of the Mount Prospect Historical Society.)

Construction began on Randhurst Mall in June 1960. In this aerial view taken in 1960, a large portion of the mall has been completed. The iron skeleton of the domed ceiling is visible, which was to be covered by concrete in order to utilize the heating and air-conditioning system proposed by Victor Gruen Associates. (Courtesy of the Mount Prospect Historical Society.)

This is an aerial view of Randhurst Mall as it looked after being completed in 1962. The store that the photograph was centered on was that of the parent company of the Rand Corporation, Carson Pirie Scott. The Fair can be seen on the left side of the picture before it was bought out and changed to Montgomery Ward a few years later. (Courtesy of the Mount Prospect Historical Society.)

This is a picture of the opening ceremony at Randhurst Mall on August 16, 1962. Randhurst Mall would cost $21 million by the time it was complete and caused multiple annexations of outlying lands by the Village of Mount Prospect. In the end, the mall would have enough parking spaces for over 7,500 cars. The mall contained a total of 28 acres of stores with a constant year-round temperature of 70 degrees. Additional features were the use of kiosks that were largely of European influence and the health care offices in the upper level. Plants gave the mall an outdoorsy feel, while light would filter through the large dome that sat atop restaurants in the center of the mall. The center of the mall was created to appear floating in mid-air as it sat between the upper level and main floor of the mall. (Courtesy of the Mount Prospect Historical Society.)

Two

Creating Woodfield Mall

Schaumburg saw that it was a necessity to open a regional mall not only to draw income, keep property taxes low, and give the people of Schaumburg and outlying areas a central shopping location, but also to help increase the size and importance of the village. In 1960, the village of Schaumburg had a population of roughly 986 with 284 total dwellings, all of which were single-family residences. The average family size of a household in 1960 was 3.4. With the first major corporations opening in Schaumburg in the 1960s, including Pure Oil in 1963 and Motorola in 1968, the village was looking to utilize the land that it had acquired through annexation to hold a large amount of industrial, commercial, and manufacturing facilities as outlined in its five-year plan. In 1967, the first multiunit dwellings were erected, which would become the first apartments in Schaumburg. These units became known as International Village and continue to exist as apartments on Algonquin Road, across from the world headquarters of Motorola. By 1969, the building of Woodfield Mall was under way as the village saw a need to create space for shopping.

At the opening ceremony, two bands were present, one of them was the Conant High School marching band. Among those in attendance were Vincent Price and Carol Lawrence. Woodfield Mall would open on September 9, 1971, just over nine years from the opening of Randhurst Mall in Mount Prospect. As Mount Prospect utilized the Kincaid Report in 1957 to aid in raising the prospect of building shopping centers to draw consumers to the area and keep residents from going outside the village limits to get their goods, Schaumburg would look to Randhurst Mall for proof of the need of a regional mall. While Randhurst was built in a triangular shape, Woodfield Mall would have a slightly different look. However, the importance of a round roadway taking shoppers along the perimeter of Woodfield Mall would play a greater role in the development of Woodfield Mall in later years. Woodfield Mall would still hold a highly geodesic look.

This outdoor sketch of Woodfield Mall shows the unique shape of various connected squares that Woodfield Mall would take. Sears can be seen on the left side of the structure with open land surrounding the outside of the mall, creating what appears to be a small town within the surrounding roadway and outline of trees. (Courtesy of DeGoyler Library, Southern Methodist University.)

The geodesic design remains a constant in this artist sketch of the J. C. Penney arm of the inside of Woodfield Mall. A triangular skylight is seen near the top of the sketch, and the storefronts and above walkway curve in and out at angles. The prominent and only distinguished characters are women wearing fashions of the late 1960s. J. C. Penney would be planned for 310,000 square feet of shopping space. (Courtesy of DeGoyler Library, Southern Methodist University.)

This architectural model of Woodfield Mall shows the continuing geodesic design, including the walkways that would cross from one side of the mall to the other, as well as between levels. With three levels, Woodfield Mall also had some plants and a small area to the left of the photograph that included a waterfall and fountain. Charles Luckman Associates would be named as the architect in 1969. (Courtesy of DeGoyler Library, Southern Methodist University.)

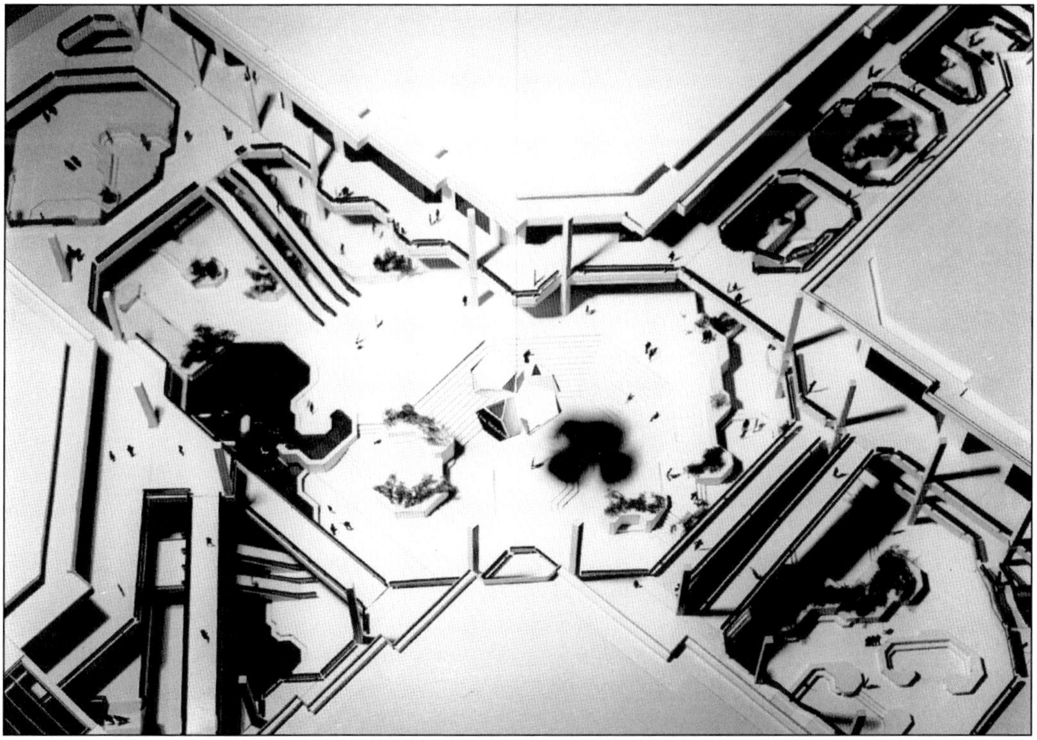

Here is a full overview of the mall in this architectural model. Woodfield mall would have four wings, each ending with one of its anchor stores. Unlike Randhurst, there was no direct path from one anchor store to the next, making it necessary to have a large number of stores between one anchor and another to maximize shopping options. (Courtesy of DeGoyler Library, Southern Methodist University.)

This is an aerial shot during construction of Woodfield Mall on September 1, 1970, just one year before it would open to the public. Construction began in July 1969, and it was developed by the Taubman Company of Michigan. The Taubman Company would not only develop the mall, but would also take over as managing company of Woodfield after completion. The Taubman Company remains the property management company to this day. (Courtesy of the Schaumburg Township District Library.)

This photograph shows Robert O. Atcher at the opening ceremonies outside of Woodfield Mall on September 9, 1971. Here he is giving a preliminary speech to all in attendance. Atcher was a country singing star of the Barn Dance on WLS radio station before he became mayor of Schaumburg in 1959. He would record over 300 songs during his career and was known for wearing elaborate shirts costing, at times, up to $250. (Courtesy of the Schaumburg Township Historical Society photograph collection/ Schaumburg Township District Library.)

This photograph shows Maggie Atcher, wife of Robert O. Atcher, in attendance of the opening ceremonies of Woodfield Mall on September 9, 1971. She would be a stage assistant during the singing career of Robert O. Atcher. Throughout his career in country music and during his tenure as mayor of Schaumburg, Maggie would be seen by her husband's side at public functions. (Courtesy of Maggie Atcher/Schaumburg Township District Library.)

Ellsworth Meineke, who was a major voice in the creation of Woodfield Mall for Schaumburg, is pictured here at the outside opening ceremony of the mall. Meineke would become a known naturist in the area as he had a bee farm and aided in the creation of Spring Valley Nature Center in 1973. He also created the Spring Valley Nature Club in 1974. (Courtesy of the Schaumburg Township Historical Society photograph collection/Schaumburg Township District Library.)

A. Alfred Taubman and his company, the Taubman Company, was the developer and manager of Woodfield Mall. He is pictured giving the opening ceremony speech inside Woodfield Mall. To his right in a white dress, Carol Lawrence listens to the speech. To the left of A. Alfred Taubman is the Conant High School marching band. (Courtesy of A. R. Trends Studio.)

Robert O. Atcher gives his speech, this time from the inside of Woodfield Mall, at the opening ceremony. To his left is Vincent Price, with hands in front of his face. Price would cut the ribbon with Carol Lawrence, marking the official opening of the mall to shoppers in 1971. (Courtesy of A. R. Trends Studio.)

Vincent Price and Carol Lawrence cut the ribbon in the center of the mall during the opening ceremony. From left to right are Ellsworth Meineke, influential board member of Schaumburg; Robert O. Atcher, mayor of Schaumburg; and A. Alfred Taubman, developer and manager of Woodfield Mall. In the background is the Conant High School marching band. (Courtesy of A. R. Trends Studio.)

Carol Lawrence takes her chance to cut a ribbon as Vincent Price (center) looks on. Months before the ceremony, Price released one of his most celebrated films, *The Abominable Dr. Phibes*. Lawrence was married to performer Robert Goulet at the time of this photograph. A native of Melrose Park, she won a Best Leading Actress award for her portrayal of Maria in *West Side Story* on Broadway in 1957. (Courtesy of A. R. Trends Studio.)

This is a publicity group photograph of some of the participants of the opening ceremony on September 9, 1971. To the far left is Mayor Robert O. Atcher. In the middle with glasses in hand is A. Alfred Taubman. Second from the right is Dr. Phibes himself, Vincent Price. Price would become an employee of Sears productions and write for the *Chicago Tribune*. (Courtesy of A. R. Trends Studio.)

A. Alfred Taubman is pictured on the right speaking with Mayor Robert O. Atcher at the opening ceremony. Woodfield Mall was named after Marshall Field, the owner of Marshall Field's, and the president of Sears, Robert E. Wood. The mall opened with 28 stores, with another 29 stores opened by the end of September, bringing the total number of stores open to the public to 57. (Courtesy of A. R. Trends Studio.)

A. Alfred Taubman is pictured on the left, with Maggie Atcher in the center, and Robert Atcher to the right. Woodfield Mall opened with the largest Marshall Field's outlying store with 330,000 square feet on two levels of retail space. The mall was created in grandeur as it boasted 20-foot-high ceilings on the main floor. (Courtesy of A. R. Trends Studio.)

Robert Atcher, on the right, gestures toward to the lot of Marshall Field's, with Ellsworth Meineke standing on his right. Despite completion of the Woodfield building structure, the dirt-covered slope suggests that there is still aesthetic work to complete. This slope would later be planted with a variety of vegetation. (Courtesy of the Schaumburg Township Historical Society photograph collection/Schaumburg Township District Library.)

Here is an aerial photograph of the area of Woodfield Mall. Woodfield Mall has been completed and outlined on the photograph with areas marked out for the development of Woodfield Plaza and Woodfield Park. Although the areas around Woodfield are largely empty, soon the land would become developed for business use. (Courtesy of Schaumburg Township District Library.)

Three

Anchor Stores

The original anchor stores at the opening of Woodfield Mall in 1971 were Sears, J. C. Penney, Lord and Taylor, and Marshall Field's. Each of these stores became the largest outlying department store of its name and are all two floors designed for maximum shopping space. Sears, J. C. Penney, and Marshall Field's all took part in developing the mall. J. C. Penney's Hobart subsidiary aided the development team in the construction, along with the Taubman Company. The name of Woodfield was created from the president of Sears and owner of Marshall Field's, Robert E. Wood, and Marshall Field, respectively.

Unlike other malls, Woodfield Mall brought four major department store chains under one roof. Each department store had its own wing of the mall, with Lord and Taylor being the fourth department store. Lord and Taylor was brought in as the fourth department store as Woodfield Mall was looking for an additional anchor that could bring in high-end products and shoppers to the mall. With the addition of Nordstrom in 1996 as part of the new Nordstrom wing that branched off the Lord and Taylor wing, the 1996 addition created a split wing with two high-end department stores.

In the early fall of 2006, Marshall Field's Furniture Galleries became Macy's Furniture Galleries. By October 2006, the department stores of Marshall Field's officially became Macy's. While the familiar structures and colors of Marshall Field's remain at Woodfield Mall, the sign marking the familiar retailer was replaced with that of Macy's following the buyout. The delivery trucks of Marshall Field's, with its forest green color and 1950s style, were simply draped with a canvas sign covering the Marshall Field's name with that of Macy's.

These anchors would hold other locations in the outlying areas, with locations at Oak Brook Center, Old Orchard Shopping Center, and Hawthorn Shopping Center, just to name a few. Randhurst Mall held just three anchor stores, which at the time would be Carson Pirie Scott, the developer and owner of the mall, with the Fair, and Wieboldt's. After just a few years of operation, the Fair was bought by and changed its name to Montgomery Ward.

The outside of J. C. Penney is seen as it appeared in the late 1970s. The top of a police car can be seen in the lower right corner of the photograph. Since its opening, J. C. Penney has not changed its outside appearance, despite recent indoor reconfigurations. J. C. Penney was one of the four original anchor stores of Woodfield Mall. (Courtesy of DeGoyler Library, Southern Methodist University.)

The J. C. Penney storefront is seen from the inside of the mall in the late 1970s. The sculpture outside the store as seen on the right side of the photograph is still standing, although the mirror structure on the left of the photograph is no longer present. The J. C. Penney marquee in this photograph does not match the artist sketch that had "Penneys" as the marquee before construction began. (Courtesy of DeGoyler Library, Southern Methodist University.)

Here is Sears as it appeared at the opening of Woodfield Mall in 1971. Sears was reported by some executives of Woodfield Mall at the opening ceremony as being a co–project sponsor for building the mall, along with the Taubman Company, although this fact has become somewhat unspoken of over the years.

This photograph was taken of the outside of Sears in the early 1980s. The signage of Sears no longer appears as seen in this picture. However, the company still operates at this location, along with the out lot automobile service station as seen to the left of the photograph. This Sears location would be the largest outlying store.

This is Sears as it appears from the inside of the mall with the more familiar signage lettering. The sculpture still exists at the storefront as it appears in this photograph. In late 1971, advertisements were run in the *Chicago Tribune* looking for various positions to fill in the mall. One such advertisement was for a coffee shop called Wimpy Grills, which was located next to Sears and Fannie Mae on the lower level.

This across-the-mall shot of Sears was taken in the 1980s. The walkways from one side of the mall to the other can be seen with pedestrians strolling between shops. Robert E. Wood played a large role in shaping Woodfield, as he was part of the Woodfield Mall namesake, along with fellow anchor store owner, Marshall Field.

This is the center of Woodfield Mall as it appeared in the 1980s. Although the center of the mall is reconfigured every so often, it remains in the current size and shape as pictured here. Trees and other plants are seen in this photograph as the mall attempted to bring a piece of the outdoors inside. In the upper right of the photograph, the fountain is partially visible. (Courtesy of Schaumburg Township District Library.)

The center of Woodfield Mall is used for various events hosted at the mall. This event in 1986, a fashion show by *Seventeen* magazine, is typical with a large crowd in attendance. Today fashion shows are still held with shoppers watching from the main floor as well as from above along the walkways and second level. (Courtesy of Schaumburg Township District Library.)

This overhead view of the *Seventeen* magazine fashion show shows the use of the raised middle walkway of the center of the mall. Shoppers sit on steps that still exist today in a theater-style configuration. The annual Christmas with Santa display and the Easter Bunny display are held in the center of the mall, making it a place of community for shoppers. (Courtesy of Schaumburg Township District Library.)

As pictured here, the display for the "World of Peter Rabbit" takes place in center court. This view is from 1993, when the Museum Store, an outlying store of the Field Museum in Chicago, began carrying Beatrix Potter's *The Tale of Peter Rabbit* for its spring collection to coincide with Easter. (Courtesy of Schaumburg Township District Library.)

Santa Claus comes to town to visit with the children in this photograph from November 30, 1988. Santa comes every year just before the Thanksgiving holiday, bringing gifts of coloring books, candy canes, and other small trinkets for his visitors. Parents can enjoy the occasion with a photograph that is available. The display occasionally is themed, as current decorations include the cast of *Happy Feet*. (Courtesy of Voice of Schaumburg Collection/Schaumburg Township District Library.)

Santa Claus's visit to Woodfield Mall on November 21, 1990, was no different than any other year. During the months of November and December, children have the chance to meet with the jolly elf of the North Pole. As shopping commences in the middle of November, Santa is ready for the number of children looking to give a hint of what they want under the tree. (Courtesy of Voice of Schaumburg Collection/Schaumburg Township District Library.)

Here is one of the Christmas displays of Woodfield Mall in 1988, entitled "Babes in Toyland." Santa would give out small presents such as candy canes or coloring books to the children who visited him. Long lines wrapped around the structure that existed as Santa's house for the season, with photographs available to parents. Here Santa's house was a carousel. (Courtesy of Schaumburg Township District Library.)

As Christmas comes and goes at Woodfield Mall, the holiday shopping is not over until the New Year sale is over. In this photograph of December 31, 1986, this mother and child are shopping for post-Christmas bargains. As the shopping bag shows, the big item for children this Christmas year was Fievel from *An American Tale*. (Courtesy of Schaumburg Township District Library.)

As mother and child shop on one end of the mall, this father and child shop at the other. On December 31, 1986, these shoppers also hunt for that New Year sale. The holiday shopping season begins the day after Thanksgiving but continues until the New Year sales are over early in January. (Courtesy of Schaumburg Township District Library.)

Bargain hunters continue to pack Woodfield Mall on December 31, 1986, as the mall continues to experience elevated sales during the nearly two-month-long shopping season. Thanks to the number of shoppers, many store locations in the outlying area depend on the holiday receipts to survive the slower summer season, such is the case of one of the remaining Toys R Us locations. (Courtesy of Schaumburg Township District Library.)

As shoppers are hunting for their holiday gifts on December 13, 1989, these schoolchildren take part in a tradition at Woodfield Mall. These schoolchildren are singing Christmas carols to the masses of shoppers during the holiday season as they gain that valuable experience of performing before a huge crowd. (Courtesy of Voice of Schaumburg Collection/Schaumburg Township District Library.)

As Santa comes to town in November, schoolchildren are in tow. Although many of the children visiting the mall are there to shop and stop in to say hello to the jolly man in red, some are there to perform. These school-age children are pictured on November 21, 1990, as they play their instruments with holiday cheer for the numerous shoppers and Santa Claus. (Courtesy of Voice of Schaumburg Collection/Schaumburg Township District Library.)

The Health and Fitness Expo comes to Woodfield Mall on May 1, 1985. Outside of Santa and the Easter Bunny, like other shopping centers, Woodfield Mall would host local and national events in an effort to draw shoppers and become a regional cultural center as well as a shopping center. The tactic has aided in creating the number one travel destination in Illinois apart from Chicago. (Courtesy of Schaumburg Township District Library.)

Holiday shopping is no longer restricted to the days between Thanksgiving and Christmas, as sales after Christmas and New Year's Day have drawn crowds comparable to those during the Christmas season. As pictured on January 2, 1985, these shoppers are part of the multitudes that visit Woodfield Mall each year for the New Year's Day bargains. It can be an exhausting task! (Courtesy of Schaumburg Township District Library.)

The Santa Claus of the spring season, the Easter Bunny makes his annual visit to Woodfield Mall on March 15, 1989. Like Santa, the Easter Bunny offers photographs for parents and small presents for the children. The display of the Easter Bunny changes on a regular basis like Santa Claus, but unlike Santa, the bunny hutch is limited to the center of the mall but is still comparable in its grandeur. (Courtesy of Voice of Schaumburg Collection/Schaumburg Township District Library.)

The alternative to Miss Septemberfest was Mr. Schaumburg. As pictured here, Mr. Schaumburg walks the runway in the center of Woodfield Mall as the village of Schaumburg is in attendance to watch its local hero. The mall attempted to mimic a small city by making the center of town the main court at the center of the mall. (Courtesy of Schaumburg Township District Library.)

Not only are mall events for children or celebrities but for the whole family. These members of the senior community take part in the Parks and Recreation Expo at Woodfield Mall. Although the major events were celebrity-attended events, or the holiday-related exhibits, the mall was truly a place for people to gather for a common purpose. (Courtesy of Schaumburg Township District Library.)

This postcard from the 1970s shows the four anchor stores of the mall. Marshall Field's, Sears, J. C. Penney, and Lord and Taylor were all major retailers at the time Woodfield Mall opened. Record sales were recorded in the early years after the opening of the regional giant. All four stores were the largest outlying stores of their brand names. (Courtesy of Aero Distributing Company.)

Another postcard from the 1970s depicts the center of Woodfield Mall. On the left is the center court with a view of the abstract square art that hung from center court. The right side of the postcard shows a view from center court of the water fountain. In the background, Marshall Field's can be seen. At the time of this postcard, there was a fish tank, much like a small aquarium, where shoppers could walk through and view fish. It was located under the fountain, with a cavelike entrance. Shoppers would also stop and make a wish at the fountain, throwing in coins, typically pennies. (Courtesy of Aero Distributing Company.)

This is how Woodfield Mall appeared in the mid-1990s. The photograph shows an outlying Woodfield Road intersection. In the background, the newly completed Zurich Towers stand tall over Woodfield Mall. The Woodfield water tower can be seen on the left side of the photograph with one of many painted patterns emblazoned on the sides. In the lower left of the photograph, open land can be seen, a site that would soon be developed into One Schaumburg Place. Although One Schaumburg Place did not last long, it was redeveloped into what is today Streets of Woodfield and still contains Maggiano's as a major restaurant and out lot building in the area. (Courtesy of Voice of Schaumburg Collection/Schaumburg Township District Library.)

Four

Schaumburg Grows

In 1970, the population of Schaumburg reached 18,730, an 18 percent increase over 1960, with 5,013 dwellings; 4,587 were single-family homes, and 426 were multifamily dwellings. The average household size fell to 3.3. Rent was an average of $225 per month, but by 1979 would increase to $220 for an efficiency, $300 for a one bedroom, $375 for a two bedroom, and $440 for a three bedroom. The circulation of the Schaumburg Library would go from 49,000 in 1966 to 446,061 in 1974, before increasing again to 662,000 in 1980. The population soared after the opening of Woodfield Mall on September 9, 1971. The population grew to 25,155 in 1972; 32,352 in 1973; 36,944 in 1974; 43,580 in 1976; 50,639 in 1978; and increased another eight percent by 1980 to reach 54,750.

To house all these people, the number of dwellings increased to 21,064 in 1979, of which 9,300 were single-family homes. Multifamily dwellings numbered 11,764, which included condominiums, townhomes, apartments, and quadroplex/coach homes. The average household size dropped again to a size of 2.6, as Schaumburg shifted from a farming community to a suburban community. The number of new building units rose from 513 in 1970 to 1,025 in 1971; to 2,011 in 1977; and finally to 1,311 in 1978 as the new housing boom slowed. At the height of new housing units in 1972, the total reached 2,791 units, the majority being apartments at 1,235 of the total. In addition, the number of new units remained high in 1973 with over 2,500 units, of which 1,094 were apartments. With the coming recession in the United States in 1974, the number of new units fell to 1,215, and then to 560 in 1975, with no new units for apartments being constructed in 1975. By 1976, the market began to rebound as 1,533 new units were issued. By 1979, the average cost of a single-family home was $87,800. In comparison, the average cost of a townhome/duplex/manor home was $64,000 and it cost just under $52,000 for a condominium or quadroplex.

The mayor of Schaumburg, Robert O. Atcher, is pictured here behind his desk. On the wall in the background is a map of Schaumburg. Atcher was very hard at work in creating the ideal community with a balance of residential and business structures. Atcher would become the builder of the village of Schaumburg in the first half of the 1970s and planner of the future of Schaumburg. (Courtesy of Voice of Schaumburg Collection/Schaumburg Township District Library.)

This photograph shows the crossroads of Main Street, which became Schaumburg Road. This photograph was taken before the paved roads of the village. Hitching posts can be seen to the left side of the photograph out in front of the two-story, two-tone house. An automobile is barely visible between the house in the left foreground and the house on the left background. (Courtesy of Schaumburg Township District Library.)

Bulldozers are ready outside of a local farm at the Schaumburg intersection of Barrington and Schaumburg Roads in 1986. Although farms remained in use until the end of the 20th century in Schaumburg, new housing and business developments were springing up at an incredible rate. Before the planned Woodfield Mall development, farmers were selling land at an average of $5,500 an acre. By the early 1970s, land was averaging $70,000 an acre. (Courtesy of Voice of Schaumburg Collection/Schaumburg Township District Library.)

On the border of Hanover Park and Schaumburg, construction was taking place as it was throughout Schaumburg Township after the opening of Woodfield Mall. Here bulldozers are ready to continue tearing up available fields for the development of housing and business. Robert O. Atcher told farmers to hold out in selling land, as his vision was not for individual homes, but large developments. (Courtesy of Voice of Schaumburg Collection/Schaumburg Township District Library.)

In this photograph, the construction of Dunbar Lakes gets underway around 1976. Robert O. Atcher is happy to have a multiunit planned urban development going up next to Conant High School, which opened in 1964. Dunbar Lakes is located on Plum Grove Road, between Schaumburg Road and Higgins Road, two of the first paved roads in Schaumburg. (Courtesy of Voice of Schaumburg Collection/Schaumburg Township District Library.)

This photograph was taken from across Meacham Road looking east and south of Higgins Road around 1986. The grassy area stands where the Target shopping center would later be planned for development in 1992. At the time, these houses were not used to having large corporations working in their backyard. Atcher's vision of residences and businesses coexisting in Schaumburg lives on as Schaumburg continues its development. (Courtesy of Voice of Schaumburg Collection/Schaumburg Township District Library.)

The Schaumburg Municipal Center opened in 1974. The center was renamed the Robert O. Atcher Municipal Center in 1995 after its second mayor and creative planner. The center houses the major departments of the village, including the mayor's office, village clerk office, finance department, and community development department. Septemberfest, which began in 1971, is held around the perimeter of the center. (Courtesy of Voice of Schaumburg Collection/ Schaumburg Township District Library.)

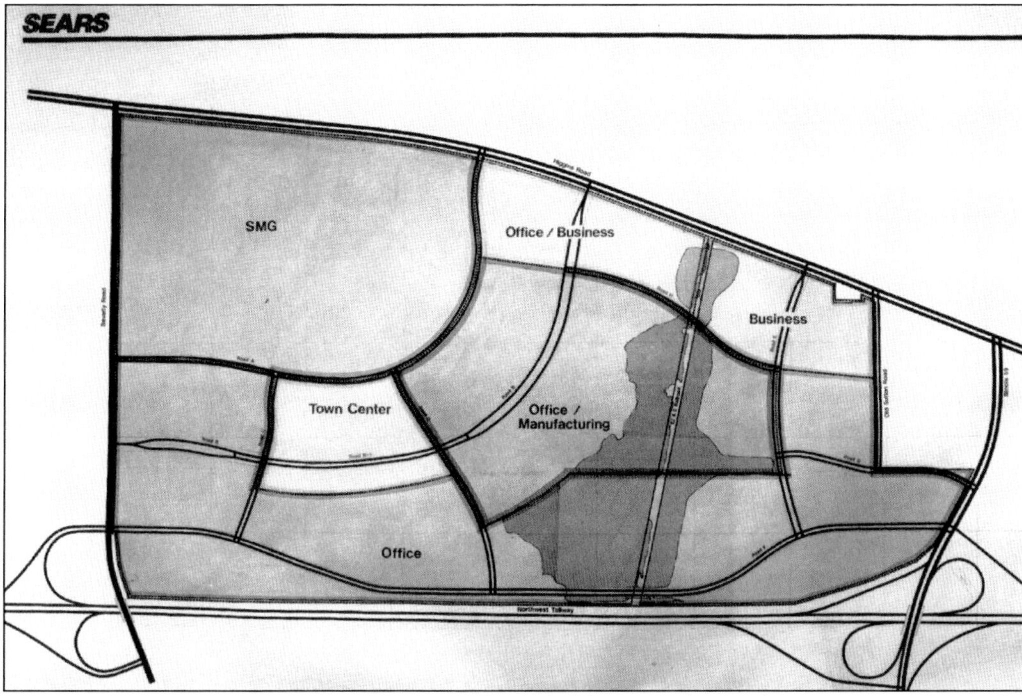

The planned Sears office development was bounded by Beverly Road, Higgins Road, and the Northwest Tollway. This area is in Hoffman Estates on the outskirts of Schaumburg; however, it was large enough to house the corporate operations of Sears. The company moved to its current location after the opening of the building in 1992. (Courtesy of Voice of Schaumburg Collection/Schaumburg Township District Library.)

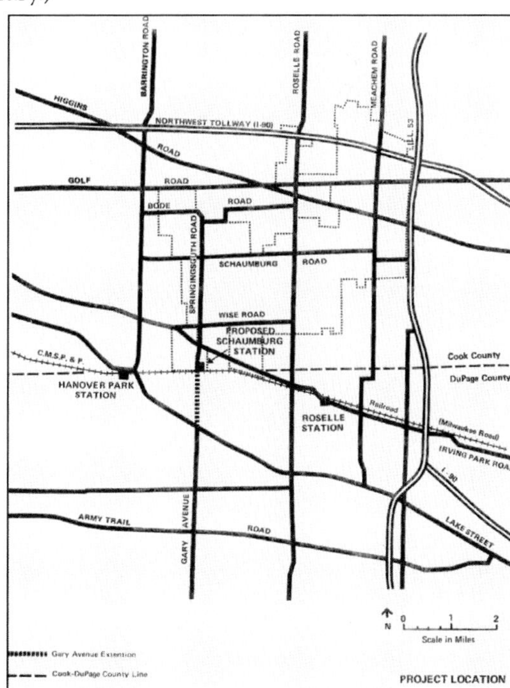

In 1979, this proposed location for a train station in Schaumburg would be the first train station for the village, marking over 100 years of expansion without the aid of railroads. Schaumburg would be a boom town thanks to road development, excellent city planning, and the construction of Woodfield Mall. The station would open in 1982. (Courtesy of Voice of Schaumburg Collection/Schaumburg Township District Library.)

This is the very first sign welcoming visitors to the village of Schaumburg in the 1970s. The byline of the sign reads, "Progress Through Thoughtful Planning," which remains the motto of the village. Nearly 20 years after the incorporation of the village, Woodfield Mall helped put Schaumburg on the map for many visitors. (Courtesy of Voice of Schaumburg Collection/Schaumburg Township District Library.)

Hotels have become a major part of the Schaumburg area as the needs of business travelers increased with the growing amount of corporations in the Schaumburg area. In Schaumburg alone there is the Chicago Marriott Schaumburg, pictured here, Courtyard by Marriott, and Springhill Suites by Marriott. All are within a few minutes of Woodfield Mall.

Zurich North America currently has its North American headquarters in Schaumburg. Each tower has 20 floors, including a dry cleaner, dentist, barber, and two eateries. Due to the height of these towers, Chicago and Arlington Park Racecourse are visible on a clear day. The towers overlook Woodfield Mall.

The American Veterinary Medical Association (AVMA) occupies a building across Meacham Road from Motorola's international headquarters. The AVMA controls the licensing of veterinary programs and is a nonprofit organization. It was created in 1863 and currently represents over 73,000 veterinarians. The AVMA also controls the accreditation of programs for veterinary assistants and technician programs throughout the United States.

Roosevelt University opened in Chicago in 1945 and then opened a second campus in Schaumburg in 1995. The university had taken the office building of the oil company Unocal over, and the Schaumburg campus remains with removable walls between classrooms as a feature that could expand office space if utilized for that purpose. The Schaumburg campus is located to the north of the Woodfield Village Green shopping center and just south of IKEA.

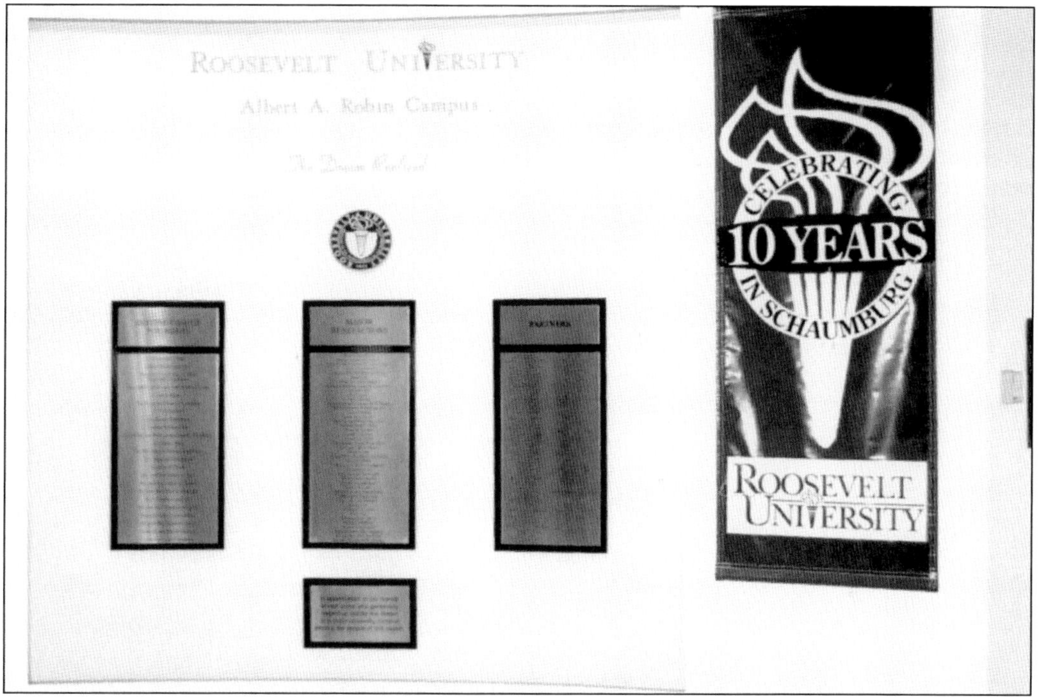

Roosevelt University is celebrating its 10th anniversary in 2006 as the Village of Schaumburg celebrates its 50th anniversary of incorporation and Woodfield Mall celebrates its 35th anniversary. Among the famous alumni of Roosevelt are Melissa Bean, Ira Brakow, Patricia Harris, Mel Reynolds, Reginald Weaver, and Harold Washington. The Schaumburg campus catered to the commuting, working adult until recently transforming into a more traditional-style university.

Harper College has been building and expanding, following the lead of Schaumburg locations. Along with the renovation of some of its buildings, the Palatine college has built a number of new facilities on its campus in order to accommodate new and expanding programs, as well as draw a larger student population.

This picture shows some of the newer structures in the Schaumburg corporate district. PepsiAmericas is currently headquartered in the building in the right foreground. It moved to Schaumburg in 2001. The building in the background on the right of the photograph, behind PepsiAmericas, is the Midwest headquarters of Verizon Wireless. To the left of the picture is the five-story Fifth Third Bank building, which also holds a branch office.

As the area grows in importance, political officials looking for voter support have found a large population of registered voters in the suburbs. Here Melissa Bean shares space with the Greater Woodfield Convention and Visitors Bureau, which has grown in importance as Schaumburg and Woodfield grow in size. The Greater Woodfield Convention and Visitors Bureau shares resources and information with companies in the area, especially with Woodfield Mall, as they help draw shoppers to the many attractions and opportunities near Woodfield.

The Schaumburg Convention Center and Renaissance Hotel was completed in the fall of 2006. The construction of this important resource for Schaumburg was long in the works as it was part of the original plans of future growth in Schaumburg. The construction of the convention center and hotel has completed the vision of growth that was originally set forth by the Village of Schaumburg.

As Woodfield Mall continues to bring growth to the village of Schaumburg, the two have made a decision to begin to make people aware that they, Schaumburg and Woodfield, are not two autonomous entities but are in cooperation. This water tower marks a movement toward making this important connection. There are at least 6 office developments that take Schaumburg as part of its name, while at least 21 take Woodfield. Office space and housing units continue to be expanded, renovated, and built to increase the available space for commerce and population that look to Schaumburg as the central location of commerce and living.

Five

A Feeling of Community

With Schaumburg growing to an exceptional size, the population expanding, and the decentralization of residents, the solely German population became more diverse. Despite becoming a sister city with Schaumburg-Lippe, Germany, in 1983, Schaumburg was no longer considered a German community and the last German-language church service took place around 1980. A piece of a stone castle from the sister city was embedded in the Schaumburg municipal center.

Woodfield Mall is a mini city and took the shape of a mini community. With trees and a waterfall, as well as light from its many skylights, the mall brought the outdoors inside. The mall created a town center with the middle court, where people would gather in a mid-mall lounging area before returning to their shopping. The mid-court was also the place to gather for events such as Santa at Christmas, the fashion shows, and guest speakers. It was a community space for the mall and its shoppers, and it became the center of Schaumburg for a number of years. The Mr. Schaumburg competition was once held in the center court of the mall.

Like Woodfield Mall in Schaumburg, other places of congregation would begin to take shape in the surrounding areas in the years to come thanks to the draw of Woodfield Mall. Randhurst Mall in Mount Prospect hosted similar events to that of Woodfield from its opening in 1962 through the end of the 1990s, when Randhurst began to lag in stature due to various reasons, but largely because of the continued draw of Woodfield Mall. Before the late 1990s, Randhurst acted as, and was partially created for, town events. Fire and police departments would have presentations for the community, trade shows would take place between anchor stores, even famous people would do autograph signings.

From the 1970s through today, various locations have appeared as meeting places for town events. Schaumburg and the surrounding areas gained notoriety as being a place for meeting the common man, the average voter, and the economic machine. The growth of Schaumburg meant growth of the northwest suburbs and the growth of the community kept pace.

International Village would be the first multifamily development built in Schaumburg. The apartment complex opened in 1968. Before 1971, the remaining units built for housing were single-family residences. In 1971, around the time of the opening of Woodfield Mall, the number of new housing units grew to 1,025, of which 11 were apartments. In 1972, an additional 1,235 out of 2,791 new units were apartments.

In 1986, the Schaumburg Marriott built the "World's Largest Snowman." Winter snow festivals took place at Woodfield Mall for many years before being moved to Roosevelt University, which has become home to the Snow Sculpture Festival in recent years. Woodfield Mall remains a large staple in the community during the holiday season. With shoppers and Santa visiting the mall starting in November, the winter spirit remains centered at Woodfield. (Courtesy of Voice of Schaumburg Collection/Schaumburg Township District Library.)

Old Towne Square opened in 1970 at the corner of Schaumburg Road and Roselle Road. The shopping center had the unfortunate timing of opening shortly before Woodfield Mall, which drew shoppers away from the limited shopping experience of Old Towne Square. This clown attempted to bring back shoppers to the center of town and the shopping center in 1980. Old Towne was bought by Schaumburg and redeveloped in 1995. (Courtesy of Voice of Schaumburg Collection/Schaumburg Township District Library.)

Virginia Hayter (right) is pictured giving a trophy mounted with cows to a recipient in Schaumburg. Hayter was a former mayor of Schaumburg. She has gone on to take part in various areas of the Schaumburg Township, including as the village clerk of Hoffman Estates. The trophy shows a slowly dying connection between the modern economic state of Schaumburg and its rural past. (Courtesy of Voice of Schaumburg Collection/Schaumburg Township District Library.)

Virginia Hayter is with Richard Elrod in this photograph. Hayter would remark on the growth of Schaumburg in the 1980s along with the necessity to do away with half of the apartment units in the village. Due to poor upkeep the units were bought by companies to rehab and resold as condominiums in order to recoup the expenses. (Courtesy of Voice of Schaumburg Collection/ Schaumburg Township District Library.)

Lincoln Federal Savings and the Moravian Cultural Society welcome the crowd gathered watching their float in Hoffman Estates. In this 1975 photograph, members of the society are wearing traditional Moravian clothes. Despite the opening of the Lincoln Federal Savings set for December 1, the parade seems to take place much earlier given onlookers wearing shorts and t-shirts in the background. (Courtesy of Voice of Schaumburg Collection/Schaumburg Township District Library.)

Conant High School marching band plays the opening of another shopping center in the mid-1970s. Hoffman Plaza was never able to pry enough shoppers away from Woodfield Mall, and sales never achieved the anticipated level. Today a Jewel-Osco is housed in the main building. Out lots in the plaza are home to Denny's, Caribou Coffee, Blockbuster, and smaller fast-food and carryout restaurants, including a Burger King. (Courtesy of Voice of Schaumburg Collection/Schaumburg Township District Library.)

Jesse Jackson gives a speech in an undisclosed location in the Schaumburg Township in 1978. Among other notable appearances in the area is Ralph Nader, who spoke at Harper College before becoming a political celebrity. Actors doing voice-overs for the *Simpsons*, movie directors, musicians, dancers, politicians, and writers have all been a part of the Harper College experience since its opening in 1971. (Courtesy of Voice of Schaumburg Collection/Schaumburg Township District Library.)

Jim Edgar knew his constituency in this 1989 pig roast visit to the Schaumburg area before he won the Illinois governor post in 1990. On his left is state representative Kay Wojcik. Wojcik would receive an honor by Harper College, where the newly constructed conference center was named after her. (Courtesy of Voice of Schaumburg Collection/Schaumburg Township District Library.)

This time Edgar (left) speaks with a marketing officer of an Elk Grove Village bank. This meeting took place at the Hyatt Regency in Schaumburg, marking another opportunity to meet with local voters. Edgar would win the governor seat in 1990 and hold the position from 1991 until 1999. He considered running for office again in 2005 before declining to run against Gov. Rod R. Blagojevich. (Courtesy of Voice of Schaumburg Collection/ Schaumburg Township District Library.)

This mother and child shop at the Hoffman Plaza, located on the boarder of Hoffman Estates and Schaumburg on Golf Road and Roselle Road. At the time, the plaza held small storefronts for shoppers. Currently the plaza is home to Jewel-Osco and still houses many small stores and restaurants, but the sidewalk sales are long gone from this corner as stores have moved to indoor sales. (Courtesy of Voice of Schaumburg Collection/Schaumburg Township District Library.)

As Ralph Nader was on the road to becoming a major political figure, he took time to stop at locations in suburbia to speak about some of his ideas. As he addressed the crowd here in Palatine, just outside of Schaumburg, at Harper College, Nader's future looked bright. He would go on to write such books as *Unsafe at Any Speed*, in 1965. He would also run in four presidential races: 1992, 1996, 2000, and 2004. (Courtesy of Schaumburg Township District Library.)

In this photograph from April 29, 1981, celebrity Monopoly was the event of the day at Woodfield Mall. Pictured here is former Chicago Blackhawk Reg Kerr, with microphone, who scored 30 goals with Chicago in the 1980–1981 season. Former Chicago Bulls fan favorite "Rush Street Reggie" Theus, current head coach of men's basketball at New Mexico State University, was second on the Rookie of the Year ballot in 1979 and is pictured to the left of Chicago White Sox great Minnie Minoso. Minoso would be the first black player in a White Sox uniform in 1951, while playing for the Sox on five separate occasions. His No. 9 was retired by the team. (Courtesy of Schaumburg Township District Library.)

Bill Kurtis came to town on one of his visits to the suburbs on July 1, 1984. Kurtis became famous as a reporter and anchor with CBS news while in Chicago from 1966 until he left for New York to become the morning news anchor for CBS in 1982. Upon his return to Chicago in 1990, he was one of the most well-known news anchors in the business. (Courtesy of Schaumburg Township District Library.)

Before the Chicago Bulls were the favorite of every Chicago sports fan, there were the 1985 Super Bowl champion Chicago Bears. The Bears were the hottest ticket in town in the 1980s. In this picture from March 4, 1987, Otis Wilson receives a warm welcome during the Bearsketball tournament at Elk Grove High School. (Courtesy of Voice of Schaumburg Collection/Schaumburg Township District Library.)

Otis Wilson and teammates take part in the tournament in this photograph from March 11, 1987. The Bears were a staple in the community, as they would go on to be a part of various suburbs and events. Walter Payton would visit many northwest suburban high schools while his son played for St. Viator High School in Arlington Heights. Mike Singletary would attend Willow Creek Church in South Barrington. (Courtesy of Voice of Schaumburg Collection/Schaumburg Township District Library.)

With their third-overall pick in the 1984 NBA draft, the Chicago Bulls would select the highest averaging scorer in NBA history. Pictured here on May 14, 1986, Michael Jordan takes part in the McDonald's basketball event at the College of DuPage. Jordan would forge relationships with McDonald's for years to come, and more importantly, he would also become well acquainted with the Chicago suburbs. Jordan would go on to bring six championships to Chicago in the 1990s, creating a new favorite team among Chicago fans, leaving the Chicago Bears of the 1980s as a part of history while the Bulls grew in popularity. (Courtesy of Voice of Schaumburg Collection/Schaumburg Township District Library.)

Before the October 26, 2006 opening of the Sears Center in Hoffman Estates, the main concert venue in the area was located in this suburb located next to Schaumburg. The current site of the Sears Center was bought in 1989 by Sears, despite Poplar Creek remaining in operation until 1994. Poplar Creek enjoyed a 14-year run, which began in 1980. (Courtesy of Schaumburg Township District Library.)

Many musicians would play Poplar Creek in Hoffman Estates. Among the acts that took the stage were John Denver and Willie Nelson. Nelson pictured here, brought his trademark oversized foam hats for fans, which left grounds crew cleaning up the aftermath of a foam-filled night after the concert ended. (Courtesy of Schaumburg Township District Library.)

In 1983, Cynthia Hodgkins won Miss Schaumburg. In 1987, she would go on to win Miss Chicago and then Miss Illinois later that year. In this photograph, current Schaumburg president, Al Larson, meets Miss Illinois Cynthia Hodgkins, in 1987. Larson would give Hodgkins a pin stating "My heart belongs to Schaumburg" when she went to Atlantic City in a bid to win Miss America. Larson became village president in 1987. (Courtesy of Voice of Schaumburg Collection/Schaumburg Township District Library.)

Lou Ferrigno visits fans at Randhurst Mall in Mount Prospect. This photograph was taken sometime in the early 1980s, around the time of the release of his book, *The Incredible Lou Ferrigno*, published in 1982. Ferrigno would play the Incredible Hulk in the television series of the same name in the 1970s and star in *Pumping Iron* with Arnold Schwarzenegger. (Courtesy of the Mount Prospect Historical Society.)

Arnold Schwarzenegger—action hero, superstar, former Mr. Universe and current governor of California—meets with fans at a signing session at Randhurst Mall. The photograph session dates from around 1977, when the release of this autobiography was published. That same year he took part in the movie about competitive bodybuilding, *Pumping Iron*, where he came out of retirement to compete again and make the film. (Courtesy of the Mount Prospect Historical Society.)

Six

The New Face of Shopping

Skokie opened Old Orchard Shopping center in 1956, which was developed by Philip Klutznick and was anchored by the Fair Department Store and Marshall Field's. In 1957, Montgomery Ward purchased the Fair, but did not rename the store at Old Orchard until 1964. The one drawback of Old Orchard was that it was, and remains, an open-air shopping center. This meant that extreme weather conditions could affect shopping. In 1962, Oakbrook Center opened in Oak Brook, Illinois, with the anchor stores of Sears and Marshall Field's. Mount Prospect would view shopping centers as a way to raise enough money to keep property taxes low. As the transportation system became more accessible to more people, a shift was made to shopping outside the village limits by residents of Mount Prospect.

As space becomes more limited due to continuing development, the question of what will happen in the housing market and to the continued entrance or expansion of the retail and corporate world comes to the front. Some of the answers are to build more multifamily units in urban developments. Apartments are once again being converted into condominiums at an alarming rate. As rehabs take place on existing buildings that have been neglected thanks to low interest rates and high home sales in recent years, many have found it cheaper to buy rather than rent. As the interest rates have increased and housing prices have skyrocketed in the area, more and more people are looking for cheaper alternatives. A move back to apartment living is an option for some, but with degraded apartments, companies are forced to sell to a major investor in order to renovate their property. These investors, in turn, rehab and recoup the expenses by selling the apartments as condominiums or townhomes to those looking for a cheaper alternative. With apartment prices once again starting to climb due to demand and high costs of purchasing a home, the renovated condominiums are selling at lower prices and have become enticing to many looking for a cheaper answer and more productive opportunity.

Cub Foods became a large wholesaler of grocery goods. This photograph of the Cub Foods shopping center in Hanover Park shows the reach of shopping centers by the time of the photograph in 1990. The wholesale grocer would lose ground in the market after the opening of Costco and Meijer in the northwest suburbs. With the parent company purchasing Albertson's recently, it decided to close the wholesale chain in Illinois. (Courtesy of Voice of Schaumburg Collection/Schaumburg Township District Library.)

A flood in 1990 in Hanover Park swamped the parking lot of this K-Mart. K-Mart became a large retailer in the 1980s and 1990s. This photograph shows what nearly all of the stores looked like. With a drop in market shares to Target and Wal-Mart, K-Mart began to close its stores, including the Super K-Mart on Meacham Road. Sears later merged with K-Mart and renamed the remaining stores Sears Essentials. (Courtesy of Voice of Schaumburg Collection/ Schaumburg Township District Library.)

The Container Store is housed in one of the large offices of the Woodfield Village Green Shopping Center, located just north of Woodfield Mall. The strip is home to more historically stand-alone stores, such as PetSmart, Borders, and Subway. The out lot stores and clusters include Circuit City, Helzberg Diamonds, and Starbucks. The shopping center opened soon after One Schaumburg Place in the early 1990s.

IKEA opened its first location in Illinois in Schaumburg, in view of I-90 in the late 1990s. It contains approximately 458,000 square feet of self-serve retail space. The store was so crowded and visited by consumers that a second store recently opened in the suburb of Bolingbrook to accommodate all the customers and alleviate the congestion of the Schaumburg location.

The coming together of town and country had taken place over a few decades in Schaumburg and came to a head in 1971. Nature and city have met more recently as the amount of open space has become nonexistent in today's suburbs. Other than nature centers and forest preserves, community colleges such as Harper and Oakton in Des Plaines have aided in saving a small part of the natural environment.

As pictured on May 3, 1989, the Pace bus that ran to Woodfield Mall was much smaller in size when compared to those running to and past the mall currently. The Pace bus is no longer the only mass transit available to shoppers and visitors to Woodfield. Tour buses flock to the mall from all over, notably from downstate colleges on weekend trips to the shopping center. (Courtesy of Voice of Schaumburg Collection/Schaumburg Township District Library.)

Unlike many of the other northwest suburbs of Chicago, such as Palatine, Des Plaines, Mount Prospect, and Arlington Heights, Schaumburg was created not from the expansion of the railroad system but of the highway system of the 1950s. This van caught on fire on October 30, 1985, while driving on I-90 near Roselle Road. During the summer months, cars can be seen along the roadway as they overheat and occasionally catch fire. The harsh and snowy winters can also claim many victims thanks to poor road conditions. With I-90/94, I-290/294, I-355, 53, and the Elgin-O'Hare, the intersection of the expressway and highway systems come to a head near Woodfield Mall, allowing access from every direction. Shoppers are able to use the roadways to travel to Woodfield from Chicago and the outlying suburbs, or on to Wisconsin, Indiana, and downstate Illinois. (Courtesy of Schaumburg Township District Library.)

This shot of the plaza behind Golf Center looking west along Golf Road shows what is currently happening to older strip malls. On the left, the only competition to Blockbuster, Hollywood Video, closed in 2006. The prices of Blockbuster down the street increased after Hollywood Video closed. This plaza contains the Melting Pot, a fondue restaurant, but is losing stores quickly.

Golf Center on the corner of Golf Road and Roselle Road, was renovated early in 2006. Among the new residents are Glass Works and a Petland/Aquarium Adventure. Michael's and Harlem Furniture still operate on the south end of the plaza, with a TJ Maxx and Card and Party between the south and north end stores.

Currently Arthur Murray, pictured at left, has just three locations, one of them being in Schaumburg. Part of the strip mall that contains the Bamboo Room nightclub was recently remodeled. The strip mall has slowly begun to become a major destination for shoppers, which has caused remodeling of many older locations. The out lots at this location off Gold Road include new buildings with Panera and Ethan Allen.

With the strip mall becoming fashionable, renovation has become important to those strips that were built prior to 2003. The move to build outward like a small village has increased the size of the land needed for strip mall space. Smaller areas of grass islands and borders between storefront and streets are suffering for the need for additional space, which has paid off in rejuvenating some areas for shoppers.

Some storefronts continually suffer from the older strip mall locations. This store location has undergone a number of retailers. As this strip mall undergoes changes to maximize the space and bring in new stores for shoppers, out lots are faring well at this location, including a Fuddruckers and Barnes and Noble, which are not pictured. Other stores continue to do well, including Kohl's.

One Schaumburg Place has made a larger transformation than any other shopping center in the area. As One Schaumburg Place lost consumers to Woodfield Mall, despite hosting local events such as autograph sessions with sports legends and housing a successful movie theater, it began to lose retailers by the late 1990s. As a result, the two-level mall underwent a transformation into a strip mall and was renamed Streets of Woodfield.

Woodfield Mall filed suit against the proposed developer of One Schaumburg Place in 1984 over traffic congestion. In 1985, the Village of Schaumburg countersued Woodfield Mall over liable antitrust law violation by the mall operators. The argument was that Woodfield was trying to keep the new $200 million shopping center, One Schaumburg Place, from moving forward. Since that time, the mall became Streets of Woodfield, with modern stores replacing traditional outlets.

By 1993, One Schaumburg Place was in trouble, with many retailers beginning the exodus. With 760,000 square feet of retail space, One Schaumburg Place added to the 7.3 million square feet of retail space in the Schaumburg area. Woodfield Mall was the focal point of Schaumburg and retailing metropolis, lending its name to the reinvented One Schaumburg Place and newly built Woodfield Village Green, a 612,000-square-foot space.

After six years of operation, portions of One Schaumburg Place were torn down. The rebuilding and resurrection of shopping, with the opening of Streets of Woodfield in 2000, gave strip malls a boost. Other retailing opportunities have entered reconstructed space, including banks such as Citibank at Streets of Woodfield.

Asha, Root, and Jamba Juice are some of the new retailers in the area. The large building behind Root is Loews Theatres. Jamba Juice opened in the face of the diet trend of the early 21st century, offering a variety of juice drinks with bases of yogurt and fruit. The juicer is a counter to the caffeinated retailer Starbucks that is offered down the strip.

Carson Pirie Scott measures in at 144,000 square feet of shopping space. A 5,000-square-foot Starbucks, not pictured, is to the right of the open space in front of Carson Pirie Scott. Chipotle is one of the only strip-based eateries available, with additional high-end restaurants available on the out lot.

Loews Theatres were originally inside of One Schaumburg Place before the mall was turned into Streets of Woodfield. The new Loews was recently bought out by AMC. The theaters still contain the original number of 20 screens from its opening in 2000. To the left of the theater, some overhangs are visible from the current restaurant, Asiago, which was originally called Dick Clark's AB Diner, opening with the mall in 2000.

Shaw's (pictured above) is part of the out lots of Streets of Woodfield, which are all restaurants, including Maggiano's (not pictured) and Big Bowl (pictured below). The current state of the modern strip mall is not to build up, but out. Bringing in major restaurants has become a major point of interest for strip malls to draw a larger crowd and increase mealtime spending given the absence of food courts as available at traditional malls. Big Bowl is one of three out lot restaurants of Streets of Woodfield. The office buildings in the background below are part of the Woodfield Business Center. In this same business district are AC Nielsen, not pictured, which is part of the Nielsen ratings company, and Marriott Hotel, not pictured.

Despite the lack of a central indoor space that is available in traditional malls, the sculptures and plants that add to the aesthetics of the shopping experience are still visible. This sculpture at the center of Streets of Woodfield is part of a small-town feeling with lampposts and benches throughout the complex to give that small-town feel. Traditional street signs give shoppers direction and add to the feel.

As Woodfield has continued to grow, so has the city of Schaumburg and the surrounding suburbs. The collision between town and nature came to a head in 1971 and has taken shape over the past decade. Open space has become almost nonexistent in today's suburbia. Along with nature centers and forest preserves, some developments have aided in preserving, or at least reinventing, a small part of the natural environment. In this photograph, one of the man-made ponds can be seen in the Woodfield Village Green Shopping Center just behind Circuit City and bordered by Golf Road. Across Golf Road sits some of the many restaurants in Schaumburg, such as the TGI Fridays seen in the background of this picture. The man-made pond in the foreground has lost some of its water level due to recent low rainfall in the past couple of years.

Seven

The Stores

Woodfield Mall opened on September 1, 1971, with just 28 stores ready for shopping. By the end of September an additional 28 stores were made available for consumers. The largest outlying stores for Marshall Field's, Sears, J. C. Penney, and Lord and Taylor were the major anchor stores for the new mall. In 1970, the fear that the shopping mall "boom" was slowing did not stop Woodfield Mall from moving forward in its construction plans. By mid-1970 a strike by construction workers halted many projects in the Chicagoland area, including Woodfield Mall. The strike was short lived, and Woodfield Mall was hardly affected. By late 1970, rising costs began to deter some developers from entering the market as the mall boom was believed to be ending. However, Woodfield Mall was on target to open in the fall of 1971.

Woodfield Theaters, on the out lot of Woodfield Mall, opened in late July 1971. With Disney characters in attendance, the two-screen theater opened with the Disney film *Scandalous John* and *A New Leaf*. Woodfield Mall opened additional movie theaters, this time within the confines of the mall itself, in 1985. The total number of screens came to nine available.

Woodfield had little competition, other than within its own walls, to worry about during the economic fears of the early 1970s, mid-1970s, mid-1980s, and early 1990s. By the 1990s, despite economic fears, this would all change. With the construction of other local malls, such as Town and Country, Meadows, and One Schaumburg Place, Woodfield began to see that there were viable competitive forces. In addition, Woodfield had to start contending with strip malls that included low-price retailers such as Target.

In 1996, Woodfield Mall decided to add an additional 500,000 square feet of retail space for an estimated $100 million, which would include the third location for a Nordstrom department store. The expansion also added an additional 1,000 parking spaces. The other locations for the Seattle-based department store would be Oakbrook Center, opening in 1991, and Old Orchard, opening in 1994.

This sign welcoming shoppers is located on the lower level of the two-level parking garage of the expansion for Nordstrom at Woodfield Mall. The Woodfield logo can be seen in the upper left of the picture. Nordstrom was added to the Lord and Taylor wing, creating a high-end wing of Woodfield Mall with two anchors.

The old North/South Road, as identified on various maps prior to this time, was renamed Mall Drive in 1970. It now intersects with Woodfield Road, marking the entrance near Lord and Taylor and Nordstrom. The out lot on the corner was home to the Curragh, which found a cheaper and larger location outside of Schaumburg. Jared, a jewelry retailer, was completed in the winter of 2006/2007.

Since the opening of Woodfield Mall, various retailers have come and gone, with the exception of the anchor stores. Woodfield Mall has become a test market for many retailers looking to enter the market, both in the nation and in the region. With 27 million visitors a year, Woodfield is a prime market place, with tour groups and buses full of college students visiting the mall on a regular basis.

This is one of the anchor stores of Woodfield Mall, Lord and Taylor, as seen from the outside. A ramp cuts across the face of this store as it leads to the two-level parking garage, which also shares access to the part of Woodfield Mall that houses the 1996 addition of Nordstrom.

Here is a view of part of the new addition to Woodfield Mall in 1996. To the right is Nordstrom. In the back of the parking lot on the left, one of the restaurants in Woodfield Mall, called Red Robin, is located. The addition of Nordstrom created an additional 550,00 square feet of shopping space and 1,000 parking spaces.

One of the more upscale restaurants in Woodfield Mall, Cheesecake Factory, brings some of the new ideas of autonomy to the mall. As malls move to bring the outdoor in and move the indoor out, Cheesecake Factory has two entrances, one on the outside of the mall, and one between entrance doors to the mall itself. This makes the entrances to the restaurant nonexistent in the mall itself.

Of the in-mall restaurants, the A&W provides unique American fare to shoppers. A. Alfred Taubman purchased A&W in 1982, expanding the chain throughout the nation and into international markets. The Great Root Bear, as pictured here, became the official mascot of A&W in 1974. By 1994, Taubman sold the company to another investor, but the restaurant remains a fixture within the mall.

Two additional restaurants, Rainforest Café and Stir Crazy, began the use of large, highly artistic signage for restaurants in the mall. Originally mall signage was very simple and plain, however, with the new wave of restaurants, the idea of large, artistic signs to bring in customers has become fashionable. Themed restaurants are also a newer invention.

This mid-mall sign for Stir Crazy features added artistic quality with a twist of technology. The sign has a miniature television showing dishes and scenery from the Asian restaurant. Unique advertising, coupled with unique dining experiences are a highlight of the new wave of dining at Woodfield Mall. Restaurants have also begun to move away from the traditional mid-mall food court and toward autonomy on the outskirts of the mall.

P. F. Chang's (left) and Texas de Brazil (right) are two of the newest additions to mall dining. More upscale and with a different mood setting, both restaurants are located on the outer edge of the mall at the end of one of the access hallways. Located across from each other in a newly renovated area of the mall, these restaurants are helping reshape the old indoor theater entranceway.

Todai, a Japanese restaurant, is one of the various ethnic-style foods in the mall. Traditionally the mall housed American food locations such as A&W, Rainforest Café, and Ruby Tuesday. In recent years the mall has added Mexican, Japanese, and Asian-infused fair. The wide range of restaurants has catered to the varying tastes of the various shoppers visiting the mall, once again mimicking a small town.

Along with the addition of upscale restaurants, upscale mid-mall snacking and an increase in candy shops have changed the face of Woodfield Mall. Lindt is one of the newest additions to the shopping experience, offering shoppers an additional source of mid-mall food and gourmet chocolate items. Before Lindt, the upscale chocolatier Godiva Chocolatier was the major retailer. Woodfield continues to bring in competing forces to foster a healthy mall economy.

This view through the Sears-centered sculpture by sculptor Robert Engman shows the two-level shopping experience of consumers. To the top right of the picture is the Finish Line, one of many sport apparel and shoe retailers in Woodfield Mall. To the left of Finish Line is one of only two photographers in the mall, the Picture People, providing portraits for interested parties.

Outside Nordstrom shoppers can view this directory of all the retailers and restaurants in Woodfield Mall. The mall directory has become a spot to locate which part of the 2.7 million square feet a store is located. Throughout the mall these signs exist and were once the main focus of locating a store of choice, now stores have their own signs, such as Stir Crazy, marking where they are located.

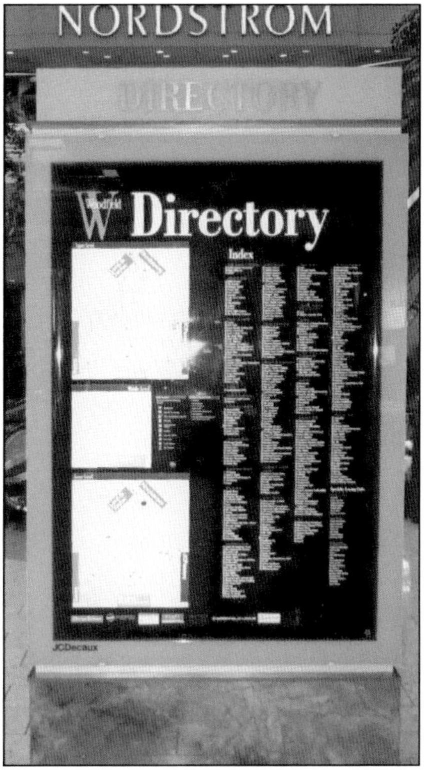

To the right of the picture is Waldenbooks, one of the original retailers from 1971. This retailer is currently located in the new wing of Woodfield Mall, near the entrance of Nordstrom on the second level. Waldenbooks had expanded their location to include a children's section as seen to the left of the picture. During the holiday season Waldenbooks adds additional retail locations in order to sell calendars.

Additions to Woodfield Mall retailers have been an increase in high-end fashion in recent years. Lacoste, pictured at right, with Bare Escentuals, and Mont Blanc to the left, are just a few of the newer locations for the high-end shopper. With space becoming a premium, some of these retailers have found a home in small corner stores or in renovated stores that were once part of a larger location.

Additional services, with a high-end connection, have also become a part of the Woodfield landscape. Pictured to the right of this picture is Mario Tricocci, with a salon location near Nordstrom. This location is only a salon location, but a full-scale day spa is available just minutes from Woodfield Mall, south on Mall Drive. There is little coincidence that the high-end salon is near the high-end department store.

Janie and Jack, pictured at the bottom of the photograph, has become the high-end fashion for the toddler shopping at Woodfield Mall. It is housed between Jessica McClintock, pictured at the bottom left, and one of the high-end make-up retailers, L'Occitaine, pictured at the bottom right. Coming soon to the location in the upper left of the picture is Cole Haan, part of Nike Inc., another high-end fashion retailer. The location becomes the third in Illinois.

As the trends in modern culture continue to evolve, so do the stores in Woodfield Mall. Pictured at the top of this photograph is the new wave in visual technology, laser eye surgery. Now shoppers can go to the mall for not only shopping and dining, but to receive medical attention. The idea of a small town under one roof is becoming reality with medical practices.

Woodfield Mall acts as a test market for many retailers, one of them being this Ruehl location. Part of the transformation of a mall is to bring the outside in. Here the storefront takes on the scenery of a city street, complete with brick facade, sidewalk, and window flower boxes in front of this high-end fashion store.

This picture shows one of the many lower-level walkways with the cart-based retailers that resemble the open-air market of Europe. Just as Victor Gruen helped create this atmosphere in the Randhurst Mall in 1962, Woodfield has also taken on a street vendor feel. To the left is the newly created C. O. Bigelow store with awnings into the "street."

Another new marketplace for shoppers, C. O. Bigelow opened earlier in 2006. This store looks like it belongs outside, with its awnings and specials board looking more antique than modern. This high-end cosmetics retailer has entered into the market of Woodfield Mall and now competes with Bath and Body Works, a lower-priced retailer that offers a limited amount of C. O. Bigelow products.

This shot from the mall parking lot shows the facade of Woodfield Mall, where restaurants create the enticing view for hungry shoppers. Restaurant signs have become a major marker for the entrances of Woodfield Mall. Other than this location, additional entrances boast Texas de Brazil, Cheesecake Factory, Ruby Tuesday, P. F. Chang's, Red Robin, and Todai.

This parking lot view offers the newly renovated location of P. F. Chang's in the background to the right with horses standing guard. To the left of P. F. Chang's is the newly-opened Texas de Brazil, a Brazilian-style steak house. To the left of Texas de Brazil is the Chicago Improv at Schaumburg, a new comedy club to the area that opened mid-2006.

The Cheesecake Factory is pictured here, the first of a growing number of upscale restaurants at the Woodfield Mall. The Cheesecake Factory is known for its cheesecake. The wait can be nearly an hour any day of the week, with peak waiting times during dinner hours on Friday, Saturday, and Sunday. The restaurant has received competition from the upscale eatery P. F. Chang's.

In mid-2006, the Chicago Improv at Schaumburg opened at Woodfield Mall. The location is the first of the mall "retailers" to have an outside-only entrance. Part of the evolution of malls, such as Town and Country, Randhurst, and Meadows, is to move from an inside-based mall to outside based, eventually eliminating the inside altogether. It is hard to picture such a trend at Woodfield based on continued interest.

Apple opened in Woodfield Mall in 2001, after the technology boom of the 1990s had already ended. However, with the rise of the iPod, Apple has found a new and continued customer base. The Sony Style store opened in 2005, offering only Sony products, from televisions and DVD players, to computers and cameras.

As with high-end restaurants, electronics, clothing retailers, and services, the mid-mall snacking venue has also become high-end, with the addition of Starbucks in the food court. Although Mrs. Field's still operates on the upper level and such snack stands as Auntie Anne's and Cinnabon are still offered, Starbuck's has continued toward one location for every 10,000 people. Only 2,698 more locations are needed for Woodfield, as Starbuck's enjoys two locations already.

One of the staples of Woodfield Mall has been the McDonald's located on the second level of the food court area. This location has undergone changes of its own, as it has created its own mini out lot by providing a bar at the front of the restaurant at the entrance, for beverages and quick treats such as ice cream.

The recently opened f.y.e has taken over the retail space of the previous retailer, Sam Goody, at this location on the second level. After filing for Chapter 11 bankruptcy in January 2006, Sam Goody was sold to f.y.e in March 2006. The store was renamed a few months later, but the layout and stock remains the same.

Hollister Company, an Ambercrombie and Fitch company, another high-end clothing retailer at Woodfield Mall along with the other Ambercrombie brand Ruehl, has attempted to bring the outdoors in with this beach cottage entrance. Hollister opened in the early 21st century at its Woodfield location and has the same familiar entrance as its other locations. Woodfield has become a testing ground for new stores like Hollister Company that cater to teenagers.

Originally the location of the service desk, construction has been underway to perhaps make way for the coming of Santa in November. The temporary location of customer service was pushed to a booth located at the end of the escalators in the middle of the mall, seen at the bottom of this picture.

This view is of the location of what were once the waterfall, fountain, and underground fish tank. The center of the mall has become the Comcast Connections Court, with a Comcast booth located at the center of the picture in the former location of the fountain. Shoppers can now purchase all their service needs, including cable. Every major wireless service provider is also available within the Woodfield Mall.

The walkway vendors offer a plethora of items, ranging from jewelry to cell phone cases to hair extensions, and Irish-related products. This vendor strip leads to the Comcast Connections Court in the center of the mall. Storefronts line the walkway as shoppers have every item within walking distance in Woodfield Mall. These kiosks have taken part of the 2.7 million square feet of retail space offered by Woodfield.

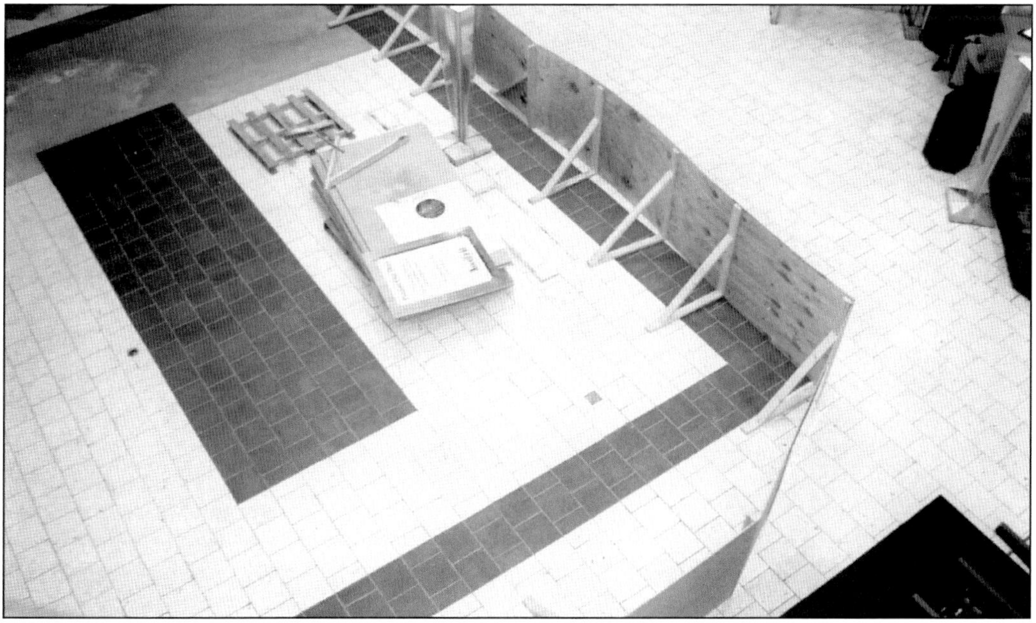

Part of the Comcast Connections Court is seen under construction in the fall of 2006. This area was once the customer service area but is currently being remodeled to create a more convenient customer service experience. In the mean time, Santa has begun to occupy part of the location and the customer service booth has been relocated temporarily. Woodfield must continue to renovate its space to make maximum use of its retail space.

The Rainforest Café is just part of the themed restaurants that have brought in diners. The size and grandeur of the location has brought the outdoors in, which is part of the life cycle of malls. The short-lived Mars 2112 restaurant, not pictured, opened in 2001 and occupied the indoor theater location. Mars 2112 took diners on a space adventure and allowed them a view of the Mars landscape while eating.

These steps once led to the "underground" fish tank below the fountain in the center court of Woodfield Mall. As pictured here, the entry way has been fitted with a locked door for storage as the fountain and fish tank have been removed from the mall experience and replaced by a Comcast booth. In the background upper right, a view of the Comcast Connections Court is visible.

These road signs near the entrance of one of the various mall roadways point in the direction of the anchor stores and the restaurants, some of the many main attractions to the mall shopper. It is difficult to tell, but Macy's covered up the name of Marshall Field's in fall 2006 as it took over the naming of the anchor store months after buying out the Chicagoland retailer.

This out lot building is part of the original structure of Woodfield Mall. This is the automobile service center of Sears, which has been in operation since 1971. Since that time a second out lot automobile service center was created on the opposite side of the mall called Firestone. This building was one of the first out lot structures to exist.

Harris Bank and the American InterContinental University have become part of the Woodfield landscape. These out lot buildings began the new wave of out lots directly on the Woodfield premises. Following the tearing down of the Woodfield Outdoor Theaters in 2000, additional buildings have gone up along the perimeter of the mall. Included in the new out lots are restaurants such as Hoolihan's and Olive Garden.

Linens and Things (above) and DSW Shoe store (below) have taken over part of the out lot space once occupied by the outdoor two-screen theaters. The out lots opened earlier in the 21st century after the theaters were torn down. The twin theaters had experienced some resurrection after the success of *Men In Black* and the later rerelease of the *Star Wars* movies, but closed before the opening of the new chapters.

Firestone is one of two automobile service centers on the out lots of Woodfield Mall. The other automobile service center is Sears. Firestone is one of two out lot structures in the northern out lot with LaSalle Bank being the other location. The large parking lots are used for overflow parking during busy times of year for the mall, as well as for the weekend bus tours and drop-offs for college students.

LaSalle Bank is the only out lot banking location at Woodfield Mall. Although Harris Bank has a building not far from LaSalle, the building acts as a corporate center rather than banking center. In the background of the picture are two of the newer buildings located across Golf Road near Woodfield Village Green. The headquarters of Assurance Agency, Ltd., the newest tenant of that building, is visible.

Eight

The Permanent Grandeur

Since the opening of Woodfield Mall there have been a number of changes in regard to retailers and products available to visitors. The one major fixture and the most overlooked part of the total experience of Woodfield Mall has been the architecture, art, size, and overall aesthetics of the mall. From the walkways and storefronts to the skylights and sculptures, Woodfield Mall is rich in scenery and visual pleasure.

The transformation of a mall becomes part of the mall experience and aids in the direction a mall is moving in its customer base and retailers. A mall begins with a very simple idea, creating a space for shoppers to come and buy all their necessary nonperishables. By adding restaurants and mid-mall food courts, the mall becomes a place for congregating and taking time to spend a day shopping. Open middle courts and other spaces allow special events to take place within this community and allow additional open space for resting from the endless amount of shopping available to visitors. The mall becomes the center of town, moving from a periphery location, which was big enough to build such a sizable structure, to becoming a hotbed of development.

As the mall takes on this role, it begins to turn itself into a small town of its own, by pulling the outside world in. Storefronts take on the shape of outside locations with sidewalks, windows, and awnings. Trees and other foliage are introduced as the skylights allow natural light to mix with the artificial lighting. The size and elaborate structures add to this experience as an artificial world is created under one roof. For Woodfield Mall the large spaces provide a number of opportunities to enhance the experiences of shoppers. With the height of ceilings, large art structures can be erected, adding to spatial sensations.

This wall structure is located outside of the mall along the circular mall road, taking shoppers all the way around the mall to search for shopping and parking. This wall extends about a block along the western side of the mall, dividing the Woodfield Corporate Centre and the Nordstrom/Lord and Taylor side of the mall.

This shot is a modern picture of the location that once overlooked Marshall Field's as Mayor Robert O. Atcher and Ellsworth Meineke stood on the roadway while the ground was still dirt. As Woodfield Mall has grown in size, there has been some outside landscaping added to create a more natural feel for shoppers and create a more concrete divide between anchors and parking lots.

This shot of the giraffe head overlooking diners at the Rainforest Café is just one of the many animals that hang out of the restaurant. Bringing the outdoors in is part of the transformation that many malls go through. The next step in the process is to begin to push the mall to the outside, notably with entrances to border stores becoming accessible from the outside only.

An alligator pictured above lies in wait at the entrance to Rainforest Café, ready to spring on unsuspecting children as they throw pennies into the pit to make a wish. The increased sense of reality creates a more natural feel to the mall, and the mechanization is a good way to create interaction between shoppers and this artificial wildlife. The leopard (bottom) is just another major figure of the Rainforest signage, while the snake to the left also moves and creates additional interaction. The Rainforest Café becomes a safari with burgers and fries. Squawking birds sit nearby as people eat their bread. Mist and a waterfall add to the experience.

P. F. Chang's entrance is guarded by two giant horses, while Texas de Brazil has a waterfall and live open flames outside its doors. The large size of the horses and torches add to the grandeur and surreal effects of the mall and the dining experience. The large size of Woodfield Mall is heightened by large objects, whether stores, ceilings, or art.

At each of the major entrances to Woodfield, it is hard to miss the large signs marking the new town that shoppers are entering. The colors and shape of the Woodfield logo have been staples of the mall as much as the sculptures that greet shoppers upon entering the community.

This entranceway to the elevator adds to the experience as shoppers are able to move from one level to the next with this elaborate glass elevator. Shoppers can look out the glass enclosure as they travel down the center of the mall, seeing in every direction the vast size of Woodfield Mall.

Part of the outdoors coming in, this tree sits at an above-average height as shoppers enjoy a cup of coffee at the café that sits below the tree and to the right of the photograph. Tables take on an outdoor café-type feel as they are surrounded by additional foliage such as bushes and trees.

The sculpture outside of Macy's has been part of Woodfield Mall since the opening. A. Alfred Taubman was highly interested in art, as he purchased Sotheby's in 1983. This sculpture was the work of Kenneth Snelson. At the widest point this structure is 24 feet with a height of 35 feet and is made of six-inch-diameter anodized aluminum tubes. The structure is held up by stainless steel cables.

This upward picture from the base of the sculpture by Kenneth Snelson shows the vast size of the artwork, as well as the geodesic shapes of the skylights that are present throughout Woodfield Mall. Snelson studied with Buckminster Fuller, Josef Albers, and Fernand Leger. Snelson has his work on display at such places as the Art Institute of Chicago, Museum of Modern Art, and the Whitney Museum of American Art.

From the center of the mall in the Comcast Connections Court, this mirror structure can be seen on the ceiling. While many do not take time to take in the grandeur of the structure and architectural work of Woodfield Mall, it is the grand size of the mall, not just the stores, that can be overwhelming for shoppers.

One of 100 original skylights at the time of the opening of Woodfield Mall, the asymmetrical octagon makes for a unique style of skylight. For shoppers, the skylight allows natural light to mix with artificial light. Woodfield began to bring the outdoors in with the use of skylights, the fountain, and some vegetation as part of the original plans for the mall.

These octagon-shaped openings allow sunlight to reach the lower level of the mall. The upper level of the mall acts as an artificial canopy much in the way a tree or an awning would, which creates an outdoorsy feel for shoppers on the lower level. With stairways and crosswalks hanging overhead, the feel of a jungle is possible although it is made of concrete and steel.

This is another overhead shot of one of the hallway entrances with skylights, showing that the skylights are actually octagonal with various geometric shapes held within the structure. Squares, triangles, and pyramids can be seen within this skylight. Helicopters originally aided in placing the skylights atop the mall. Helicopters also aided in putting new air-conditioning units on top of the mall as recently as the summer of 2006.

This photograph shows the two-level structure of the largest outlying J. C. Penney location, with one of the mirror sculptures that once graced the open space of Woodfield Mall. The geometric-shaped lounging area to the right of the structure highlights the continued use of geometrics in the shaping of the architectural outlay of Woodfield Mall. At the time, red was used to cover the bench cushions in the resting areas along with a dark yellowish color in some locations. (Courtesy of DeGoyler Library, Southern Methodist University.)

This skyward shot of the structure outside of J. C. Penney is made of steel-plated, baked enamel. It was constructed by Robinson Fredenthal, giving it a geometric illusion with its 24-foot-high and 6-foot-square structure. He was encouraged by Robert Engman in his work, especially with this piece. Engman would create the Sears sculpture with 3,500 pounds of stainless steel and an aircraft cable spanning 24 feet high.

A full shot of the Robinson Fredenthal sculpture is seen outside J. C. Penney. A. Alfred Taubman was a shopping mall magnate but also enjoyed artwork. It is no wonder that three of the major anchors received a major art piece to be located outside their entrances. Woodfield Mall became a project of architectural wonder. Robinson was educated at the University of Pennsylvania, receiving bachelor of arts and bachelor of architecture degrees.

This water fountain marks one of the main entrances to the Marshall Field's store. The benches for shoppers to rest by the fountain are in the traditional forest green color. Despite the recent name changes for Macy's stores, the benches remain this same traditional color. Small potted plants can be seen around the fountain.

This picture of the current Macy's store, formerly called Marshall Field's, shows the size of the Kenneth Snelson structure, with the walkways crossing in front of the art piece. The trademark archways of the former Marshall Field's store are visible in the background of the entranceway of the department store. The outlying furniture gallery on the opposite corner of Golf and Meacham Roads was renamed a month before, also retaining the same archway structure.

Even the garbage cans and resting areas are of the same geometric design as the rest of the mall. The marble resting place marks the entrance to the Lord and Taylor and Nordstrom wing of Woodfield Mall. The garbage can remains the same octagonal shape as the octagonal skylights covering one half of the mall.

The architects went as far as using a geometric shape for the glass elevators and the elevator structure. The walkways and stairs also resemble geometric shapes, making the whole of Woodfield Mall a work of geometric art. The skylights and mounted lighting are also in the same design, with the center court of the mall taking on the same structural features.

Woodfield continues to make sure that shoppers see that they are entering Woodfield Mall, with the sign available at most entrances to the retail outlets and restaurants inside. This sign is seen above a rather large horse, showing that the mall is much greater in size in order to dwarf this 12-foot-high statue.

This aerial view of the outside of Woodfield Mall from 2006 shows the current expanse of the mall and outlying area. As Woodfield continues to grow and renovate itself to appeal to more shoppers, the outlying area continues to grow and renovate at the same rate. Woodfield Mall has become the main force behind the growth of the economic landscape in the northwestern suburbs of Chicago.

BIBLIOGRAPHY

Armistead, Betsy and the Village of Schaumburg. *Schaumburg*. Charleston, SC: Arcadia Publishing, 2004.

Cohen, Lizabeth. *A Consumers' Republic: The Politics of Mass Consumption in Postwar America*. New York: Vintage Books, 2003.

Duany, Andres. *Suburban Nation: The Rise of Sprawl and the Decline of the American Dream*. New York: North Point Press, 2000.

Durston, Ellen. "Mall Reborn as Main Street: Streets of Woodfield Jazzes up Old Notions of Retail Centers." *Chicago Tribune*, March 1, 2000, sec. 9.

"Fields Unveils Its Largest Outlying Store, in Woodfield." *Chicago Tribune*, September 9, 1971, sec. 3.

Hartshorn, Truman A. *Interpreting the City: An Urban Geography*. New York: Wiley, 1992.

http://en.wikipedia.org

http://www.chicagoblackhawks.com

http://www.chicagohs.org

http://www.deadmalls.com

http://www.shopwoodfield.com

Ibata, David. "Schaumburg Land Squabble Comes to End." *Chicago Tribune*, December 10, 1985, sec. 3.

Kleespies, Gavin. *Lost Mount Prospect*. Charleston, SC: Arcadia Publishing, 2006.

——— and Jean Powley Murphy. *Mount Prospect*. Charleston, SC: Arcadia Publishing, 2003.

Nebel, Fred. *Daily Milk Delivery Log to Fred Nebel of Nebel's Corners, 1890–1892*. Elgin, IL: Advocate News Book and Job Printing and Book Binding House, 2002.

Northwest 2001: A Report to the Northwest Community, October 19, 1988. 1988.

Schaumburg Business Association. *Schaumburg, Illinois: Community Profile*. Schaumburg, IL: Village Profile Publication, 1980, 1983, 1996, 2000, 2002, 2003, 2005.

"Schaumburg to Begin Shop Center Work." *Chicago Tribune*, October 4, 1969, sec. 2.

Souter, Janet, and Gary Souter. *Arlington Heights: Downtown Renaissance*. Charleston, SC: Arcadia Publishing, 2001.

"Woodfield Mall to Host Biggest Stores." *Chicago Tribune*, May 24, 1970, sec. 3A.

Discover Thousands of Local History Books Featuring Millions of Vintage Images

Arcadia Publishing, the leading local history publisher in the United States, is committed to making history accessible and meaningful through publishing books that celebrate and preserve the heritage of America's people and places.

Find more books like this at
www.arcadiapublishing.com

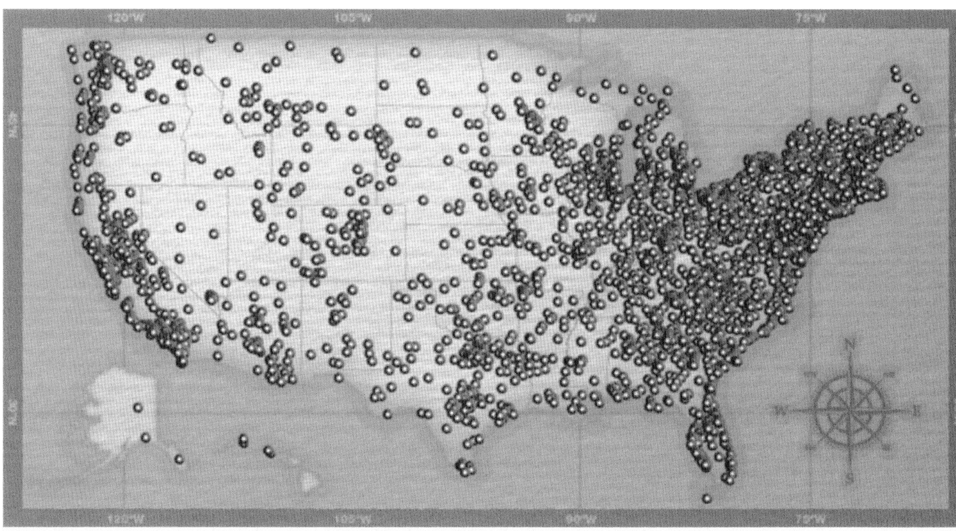

Search for your hometown history, your old stomping grounds, and even your favorite sports team.

Consistent with our mission to preserve history on a local level, this book was printed in South Carolina on American-made paper and manufactured entirely in the United States. Products carrying the accredited Forest Stewardship Council (FSC) label are printed on 100 percent FSC-certified paper.

MADE IN THE USA